T0209430

"Try as we might to evade it, we all must eventually look death in the eye. The thought of life as we know it ending is frightening to many, if not most of us. Ellen Stilwell helps to soothe the souls of those facing the end of life and guide them as the end nears. As importantly, Ms. Stilwell helps friends and relatives of persons who are dying to understand and accept the process. In *Love Death Love,* Ellen gives guidance to those whom she cannot help in person."

- J. GAIL BANCROFT

"Ellen Stilwell, by fate and choice, swims the deep waters of our uncherished birthright: death. Her encounters as a wife, sister, friend and hospice nurse exemplify her observation that 'this kind of love never dies.'

Love Death Love, beautifully written and heartfelt, is a valuable companion on the bookself next to Byock, Nuland, and the Levines."

- KIMBERLY HONE, RN
Certified Hospice and Palliative Care Nurse

"If you have ever been touched by the reality of death and grief, then this 105 page gem of a book will earn your respect

Praise for...

Love Death Love

"The words in this treasured, thoughtful book came to life recently for me as I struggled to care for my sister, Arlene, who was dying from Stage 4 colon cancer. Through Ellen's guidance, I was able to care for Arlene with right action attending to her physical, emotional and spiritual needs.

Ellen is that rare combination of a gifted medical professional and spiritual advisor who goes on the journey of helplessness and loss with you and somehow is able to help restore you to wholeness at the end. Her words help you to survive."

— VIRGINIA DALY, Caregiver

"Ellen generously shares her journey as she struggled with her husband's death. She also writes of her hospice work with patients from various traditions and beliefs. This book is a gift to anyone grappling with the coming death of a loved one or of one's own approaching death."

— MAUREEN O'LEARY, LCSW

and gratitude. Ellen Stilwell presents a collection of insights, traditions and hard-won personal experience that will guide you to feel more deeply connected with our core existential challenges, and even taste the possibilities of comfort, meaning making and post-grief growth."

- MATT MORSE, Bereavement Counselor

"*Love Death Love* shares one person's courageous journey through one of life's most difficult challenges, the death of one beloved. The author's search for meaning surrounding her tragedy and her eventual acceptance of its outcome leaves her more whole spiritually and filled with love and healing. Her story is a universal one. Reading this lovely book may have the power to help others through their own grief and bereavement."

- M. M. SQUILLACE, MD MPH HMDCB
Hospice Physician

"Ellen Stilwell shares the wisdom and grace that she has received and generously given in her years of professional assistance and pastoral care for the terminally ill. Her book should be in the pocket of every nurse and hospice chaplain."

- Fr. MICHAEL HILBERT, S.J.

"This book is truly a work of love on behalf of those who mourn the loss of love. No small gift to our human community. Ellen has a gift for clarity and distillation of fearlessly felt emotions. The result is an affirmation of faith and human resilience."

- ANTHONY MISERANDINO, Ph.D.,
Fordham University, Educational Leadership
Program, Administration, and Policy

"Ellen's tone is gentle and kind, but at the same time realistic. The stories bring out the main insights and experiences that the author wants to share with her readers in a clear manner. I found this book to be helpful not only in going through the passing of close family members and the feeling of loss afterwards, but also for when thinking about my own inevitable passing. The book is short and easy to read, but filled with wisdom. I especially like the list of short points and summaries at the end of the book under the heading Helpful References."

- JOHNNY FLYNN, Educator

BOOK REVIEW

A debut volume of true stories explores the myriad facets of loss and grief.

"Stilwell asserts at the beginning of her slim book that she's extremely experienced when it comes to final care and death. She was taught by a Buddhist monk/hospice chaplain to be a death doula, a kind of trained companion for somebody who's going through a momentous health change. The author was raised Irish Catholic, became a registered nurse, and is now a certified hospice palliative nurse, skilled at helping patients and their loved ones through the ends of their journeys. She makes clear that she's also well acquainted with death in her personal life, and her book is intended to distill all that suffering—as well as the happiness and serenity—into a series of stories and insights that might help readers going through similar things. Stilwell fills the volume with her own experiences: the losses of loved ones and relatives, the various jobs she's had, and so on. This autobiographical strand continues through her reflections on various patients she's known, individuals whose backgrounds stretched across many religions and cultures, from a spry, older Jewish woman to a Muslim refugee from Yemen. A wealthy, cantankerous woman named Gertie was brought gradually over the course of months to a peaceful acceptance of her own impending death, and Stilwell writes how she felt herself transformed by that recognition. These and other stories are told with an affecting simplicity that neither cloys nor preaches. The hard realities of the hospice experience are present on every page, but so, too, are the author's compassion and faith in the value of simple connections. These tales are touchingly filled with little details: whispering with a sick individual in the mornings; sitting with patients while they remember their intricate lives; hearing people's final attempts to make sense of their complicated family relationships. Readers who have been through the palliative care experience will be quite moved."

— *Kirkus Reviews*

Love Death Love

Ellen Long Stilwell

BALBOA.PRESS
A DIVISION OF HAY HOUSE

Balboa Press books may be ordered through booksellers or by contacting:

Balboa Press
A Division of Hay House
1663 Liberty Drive
Bloomington, IN 47403
www.balboapress.com
844-682-1282

Because of the dynamic nature of the Internet, any web addresses or
links contained in this book may have changed since publication and
may no longer be valid. The views expressed in this work are solely those
of the author and do not necessarily reflect the views of the publisher,
and the publisher hereby disclaims any responsibility for them.

The author of this book does not dispense medical advice or prescribe the use
of any technique as a form of treatment for physical, emotional, or medical
problems without the advice of a physician, either directly or indirectly. The
intent of the author is only to offer information of a general nature to help
you in your quest for emotional and spiritual well-being. In the event you use
any of the information in this book for yourself, which is your constitutional
right, the author and the publisher assume no responsibility for your actions.

If you would like to reach out to the author, use this email address:
lovedeathlove.els@gmail.com
Or, Website
http://www.EllenLongStilwell.com

Print information available on the last page.

ISBN: 978-1-9822-4330-2 (sc)
ISBN: 978-1-9822-4331-9 (e)

Library of Congress Control Number: 2020902913

Balboa Press rev. date: 06/08/2021

DEDICATION

To Family Members

Tina, Lindsay, Stanley, Troy James, Stanley John and Austin

How Much Time is There...

Accepting the Journey to Death

This book is for readers who are dealing with grief and pain while facing an end of life experience. An easy-to-read book like this is likely all he or she would want to read at such a time.

I hope this book will help that reader.

Please read on...these pages reflect my own experiences. I hope that you can relate to something in them in a way that lightens the pain or prospect of death, allowing you to cherish your remaining time together and to help your loved one accept what is happening.

CONTENTS

Chapter I   My Experience 1

Chapter II   Your Experience 6

Chapter III   The ICU 14

Chapter IV   My Sister's Family 18

Chapter V   My Husband's Discovery 23

Chapter VI   It's Really Just Love 35

Chapter VII   A Muslim Patient 39

Chapter VIII   Catholic Guilt 43

Chapter IX   A Beautiful Journey..............................47

Chapter X   Peace...52

Chapter XI   A Mother and Eldest Daughter 55

Chapter XII   The Lovers 60

Chapter XIII   Grief.. 64

Helpful References 69

Prayer/Ritual References 75

Messages For Loved Ones 91

Additional Resources 99

Acknowledgements 107

CHAPTER I

MY EXPERIENCE

"How much time do I have? How much time do we have?" These are the first questions we ask when we or a loved one receives a terminal diagnosis. From that moment, everything changes. The cascade of emotions is felt and denied at ever-changing intervals. Learning to accept death as part of life can be as natural as accepting the birth of a baby. Through the journey to death, time becomes a factor until it is not; and its importance seems to evaporate. When love is a part of your experience, time is less important, as it becomes about the journey.

I have been trained by a Buddhist monk/hospice chaplain and hospice social worker to be a death *doula*. I was raised an Irish Catholic, became a Registered Nurse, and am now a Certified

Hospice Palliative Nurse. I learned to live and thrive in New York City, a place with people from every culture, religion, sexual orientation and social status.

You may be suffering your first deep loss. My heart goes out to you. If you are the one dying, you are having a firsthand experience. Honor yourself. Pull from deep within the courage that you need. It is there….

I have had many experiences with people dying, and I have become more adept at helping with the journey. I know that when it is my turn I too will experience fear, but then I will also know peace and serenity, because of my trust and faith that I will be surrounded by love when my heart stops. Furthermore, with acceptance, this love can be received, and often is.

My father died in 1990, six months before I married my husband, Stanley. Lindsay, my six-year-old niece, died in 1991, my mother in 1992. Tina, my younger sister, passed away at age thirty-one in 1993, her husband in 1995. My dear husband was diagnosed in September 2000 with pancreatic cancer and died in March 2003. Michael, my oldest brother, passed over from his second heart attack in 2005. Two of my brothers-in-law died in 2012. Their suffering, and my suffering, has taught me much that has made me stronger, and able to give and receive love.

There can be beauty surrounding the process of dying. It starts with acceptance. To get to acceptance, become aware, honor and acknowledge your fear. You may not even know that you are fearful. It may be expressed in anger, withdrawal, isolation, self-pity, alcohol abuse or opiate use, overeating, not eating, denial, or hiding behind busyness or blame of others or yourself.

It is all about being aware of your feelings. Let go of the negative and embrace positive feelings. What would you have to lose at this point?

I have searched within myself and rethought my experiences to learn why some patients and families have the gift of acceptance. An open mind is key as is resolving resentments between loved ones. Having someone trustworthy at your side who is not frightened of the death process is a benefit. This allows those involved to let down their learned defenses and allow love to flow. God is love. If the notion of God is uncomfortable for you, focus on the love. Love brings peace. When we can accept love, we can welcome death, and know that all this is part of life.

I was born with faith and have always loved deeply. For the longest time, I believed everyone had faith and love in their life. Then the reality of life seeped in. The innocence of my faith and love was challenged by the grief that comes with the reality of life. Through the "dark nights" of my soul, every step I took was endured and ultimately transcended.

My faith is stronger now than it ever was. My love for myself and others is deeper. My experience has shown me that one can accept death through love, faith, and trust, but it takes understanding.

CHAPTER II

YOUR EXPERIENCE

Everyone handles death in their own way and at their own pace. Allowing the progression to unfold personally helps us through the various emotional stages surrounding death and dying.

Early writings of Dr. Elisabeth Kübler-Ross explain denial, anger, bargaining, depression and acceptance as stages that patients and caregivers experience. I was influenced by her book, <u>On Death and Dying,</u> which I read when my sister was diagnosed. These five stages may or may not occur in any order.

The emotional pain of knowing you will soon die or that a loved one is suffering from a fatal diagnosis can be hard to bear. **Denial** is a defense mechanism used to avoid painful but natural emotions and painful life events. Manifestations of denial may be submerging yourself in work and being so focused on producing that there is no time to think about illness and death. Some people take academic courses, bake, cook, eat, exercise, laugh, drink, do drugs, become angry, have sex, participate in extreme activities, isolate themselves and focus on anything but the pain of the diagnosis. Denial is a primitive defense mechanism that works well and can work for a long time. Sometimes too long.

Family and friends being in denial is extremely difficult for the ill person. Being the person moving toward death with no one around accepting and acknowledging it, is lonely and confusing, like ignoring the pink elephant in the galley kitchen. No one is talking about it. Are they?! They think they're protecting their loved one, but they are not.

Allowing **anger** to come up and out is cleansing. "Why me? The results are wrong." Anger toward the medical profession is common. You want multiple opinions to prove the doctors wrong. Anger toward loved ones for little things is common. Also, being angry at the individual dying *for dying* is possible and should be acknowledged.

The person dying may **bargain** with God to be a better person in exchange for the disease disappearing. Wondering, "What have I done wrong? I've done everything right during treatment." Some become kind and generous when they were not before.

Depression is a principal stage of facing death. People dying often descend into their sadness and, discover, "This is *!x!#* true!" This is not a dream. This is a living nightmare. "What am I going to do? I am scared." Anger and fear feed the depression.

The solution is in the **acceptance**. Realizing the truth of the situation sets up the spiritual synchronistic events that follow. Believing that death is coming allows the beauty of that fact to unfold. Imagine a bud about to open with all its wonder, color, texture and scent, and then it blooms. This is the essential nature of life. There is a garden around you that supports your process, whether the present moment is a thunderstorm of grief or a sunrise of serenity and surrender. Accepting the inevitable can be beautiful and productive; not accepting it is tragic.

This is a choice for the living too. I remember my mother saying, "I am going to live until I die." Everyone will die. It is something that we all have in common. When you are ready to accept that you are dying, when you are ready to accept that your loved one is dying, the peace that surpasses understanding will carry you. This will occur only if you allow it to happen.

This will be painful. It takes courage and perseverance to acknowledge your feelings and emotions. To be conscious of oneself and those around you is advantageous. It is best if you have a team of friends and family supporting you and one another.

A deep and loud scream was helpful to me when I felt the most inadequate with this totality. I went into the woods to be alone. I cried aloud for a long time until my angst was all out. What happened after this was like a subtle divine intervention. I was helped. I was relieved of a lot of emotional negativity. And could go on....

A common question is "How much time do I have?" Time is linear moving from the past into the future. Death is a part of life. Our soul goes on...until there is no time. Once our heart stops, we are free to soar. The shell of a body is shed and we are free to continue with love. Accepting death in this way brings peace and allows everyone involved to participate in the beauty of the journey to death...together, comforting, trusting, being present, feeling the pain, moving from an anxious hanging on to a peaceful letting go. Transcending into knowing that our souls continue without time. Through acceptance we find peace, in peace, we discover love.

I have no lock on THE truth. I only know my experience - my own and what I have witnessed of others'. It is quite possible that others have other paths and truths that they find deeply meaningful. I find that when I listen, really listen, to another's sense of their experience, something transcendent seems to happen. We are not alone. Others may not use the same language to describe it. However it is described, when I have experienced it, it has been uplifting, even in the face of death. I think of it as love.

I am a hospice nurse.

This is my experience, over and over.

But to get there I would propose letting go of false beliefs. We have developed them from our parents, their childhood experiences, our childhood experiences, fears of which we are not aware, and the visceral sense that we are not safe. You <u>are</u> safe. You are <u>not</u> alone.

I would encourage you to be open to growth, and transform buried fear into love and childlike trust and faith that you are not alone. Trust that dying is just like the process of birth. We all will die. Yes, some are closer than others, but why put up barriers? Fear is why, fear of the unknown.

Religious belief may help now. Unfortunately, though, it may taint the purity of the dying process. Negative teachings, internalized in childhood in many of us are hard to let go. LET THEM GO. All is forgiven…. ALL. I don't believe there is a hell. Quite possibly you have already felt singed by the fire and brimstone. If culture could see death and life as interwoven, dying will not be so intimidating. It will become tolerable. Old beliefs will be remedied. Why wait to be so exhausted by the fight to stay alive?!

Is everyone involved exhausted by the fight? Is the dying person wishing for death yet? Do you (dying person and/or caregiver) feel guilty for wanting relief in death? Do you feel helpless in leaving your loved ones? Have you prayed that the suffering will end?

If you do not believe that there is much more to life than being merely human, this would be a good time to contemplate your mortality. If you allow the prospect of death, it brings growth. Embrace your fear in order to conquer it. Feeling profoundly alone for a sustained period of time helped me to tap into the fact that I am never alone. God and my loved ones are right there. God is love. You are love.

Did something ever happen to you that just could not be rationally explained? Did this require simple acceptance? Think back on your life. What has happened that cannot be rationally explained, that made you think, "Now, that was odd." There are many different levels to this. Coincidences occur very often. The more I'm aware of them the more they happen. This changed my perspective on life. My mind became more open to events that helped me believe there is more to life than meets the eye. There are vibrations and energy of which I can become aware. Love is an energy.

CHAPTER III
THE ICU

In my twenties, I worked in medical intensive care and surgical intensive care. I was not prepared for the amount of death I saw. In nursing school there was no class to prepare us for death and dying. I had to learn by experience. The care I witnessed often seemed to simply be extending the process of death. Medications like dopamine is often calibrated and dripped into the bloodstream to maintain blood pressure. This keeps the patient alive and I felt a heavy responsibility to keep patients alive. The physician would write the order, the pharmacist would send the dopamine, and I, as a nurse would administer it. Sometimes more than one medication was needed to continue a heartbeat, sustain the blood pressure, and keep the kidneys working. This could go on for days, weeks, and sometimes months when the person was on a respirator all the while, with no response. <u>Usually</u> no response, that is....

I remember one night shift in the surgical intensive care unit when a ninety-six-year-old gentleman who was not on a respirator but was on low drip dosages. His family had recently signed a DNR (Do Not Resuscitate) order. His breathing was congested and sometimes absent. I wanted to suction him to relieve him of the secretions inhibiting his breathing. The documentation stated that he was unconscious, and he appeared that way to me. As I was about to suction him, his rather large hand firmly grasped my wrist. I was so shocked. His eyes opened slowly and he looked at me as if to say, "Please don't." He died within the hour.

A twenty-two-year-old man was being kept alive by IV fluids and medications. He'd been involved in a bar brawl days before, and a blow to his head had left him brain dead. His mother was approached by the organ donation team. I was deeply impressed with her clarity, courage, and generosity. She made the difficult decision to donate her son's organs. We had to keep his organs vital until they could be harvested and helicoptered to the recipients. From these moments of desperation and sadness come many gifts of life to others. I'll never forget the sound of the helicopter as it left in the middle of the night.

When I was a floor nurse, and someone died, a full code usually was conducted, with CPR (Cardiopulmonary Resuscitation), boluses of drugs given, and intubations. But that was before I was an ICU nurse and did not know what followed. Apparently, the goal was to keep the patient alive at all cost, but what quality of life did this provide? Through these experiences I came to realize that all this medical intervention most often just prolonged death…so who is it really for?

I believe acceptance of the inevitable is healthier and more humane.

CHAPTER IV

MY SISTER'S FAMILY

My little sister, Tina, died from AIDS in 1993 which had been diagnosed in 1985. She had been infected by her husband, Omar, who had a history of heroin use. Sadly, their daughter, Lindsay, was also diagnosed with HIV at age one. All three discovered that they were HIV+ at the same time. This was devastating. Lindsay died in 1991 and Omar died in 1995.

They all were in clinical trials for medications now used for the treatment of HIV. They participated in extensive research groups in the early days of the disease. It became Tina's life mission to thoroughly follow protocol created by the NYU/Bellevue research team. There were periods of hope and then disappointment. In the end there was gratitude to have been part of the pioneering generation for the treatment of AIDS.

Three days before Tina died she and I were seated in chairs at the end of her bed. She explained to me that she felt that it was time to let go of her body. It was getting too heavy. "I want to soar," she said. She wanted to let go of "this shell." Tina was also asking me to let her go because I was trying to keep her here. I couldn't help but understand what she was expressing to me. It had been a very long and difficult fight. She was ready to go and she wanted me to be ready too.

I now reflect on what a wonderful sister she was for thirty-one years. She was my best friend and my soulmate. She taught me much of what I know regarding death. Detaching from her caused deep and painful heartache that I felt it to my soul. This was when I became inexorably aware of my own soul. I'd felt similar pain previously, in 1990 and 1992 when my parents died, but I was not then conscious of it. It was the soul connection I had with Tina that helped me to be more aware of my spirit. I now do not have to experience severe sorrow to know I have a soul, a soul that is the love connection to all. This love never dies. Unconditional love is a constant. I can draw on it when my chakras are clear and also when I am trying to become emotionally balanced. All I have to do is ask. Ask whom, the universe, God, myself, creation. Whatever name you give it. Just have faith and trust that help is on the way.

Tina's daughter Lindsay's passing over was beautiful and permeated with her joy and love! At six years old she was in pediatric ICU, and everyone was there for her. She was cheerful and playful! We were told that her death was imminent. System by system slowed to a stop, but oddly she was conscious and aware of everyone present. She noticed that her mother's cousin was not in the room and asked for her. That made the cousin delighted to go in and be with her for a little fun and frolic. Without any discomfort, Lindsay closed her eyes and stopped breathing.

I feel deeply, and am convinced that this child's, short but impactful life, full of joy and wisdom, was her fate. The same holds true for Tina.

P.S. The summer following Tina's death I visited my older sister, Karen, in Seattle, Washington. Karen's best friend gave me the book <u>Many Lives, Many Masters</u> by Brian Weiss. I could not put it down. It was incredibly helpful to me in my grief. Perhaps you too may want to read this book. It is about past-life regressions and is captivating and comforting. Years earlier my interest had been sparked by reading books by Shirley MacLaine and Marianne Williamson that also mention this practice of past-life regression. My library of books have grown to include many more authors. For example, Deepak

Chopra, Anthony de Mello, Eckhart Tolle, Thich Nhat Hanh and Viktor E. Frankl.

Weiss's book showed me that my love for Tina was strong, not just because she died young, but because we are souls traveling together. Our love for each other will never end, although our human incarnations must.

P.S.S. It is helpful for me to remember my sister as she was when she was healthy.

CHAPTER V

MY HUSBAND'S DISCOVERY

One day after Stanley, my forty-six year old husband, woke up I noticed that the whites of his eyes were yellow. The results of a CT scan done at 10AM on September 27, 2000 revealed that he had pancreatic cancer. Oh, my God!

We went to Memorial Sloan Kettering Hospital for a second opinion. The results were the same. Some good news though. It was not an adenocarcinoma, but a carcinoid. Carcinoid is a hormonal cell type that is not as vicious as adenocarcinoma. But further testing showed that the cancer had metastasized to the liver. Chemotherapy and radiation followed.

This turned our lives inside out. I cannot imagine what was going on in Stanley's mind, but we were supportive of each other. Shortly after the diagnosis we went upstate to hike in the woods. This was a favorite pastime of ours. We packed a lunch and spent the day with our children, walking and talking. By this time, I had read many books about metaphysical Eastern philosophies that I did much of the talking. Stanley said, "Keep talking, El, I am listening." I continued speaking about how we choose our parents before coming into this lifetime (one of numerous "lifetimes" in Hindu philosophy), and the experience that we will have. He said, "I don't know why I would choose this fate." I persuaded him to go off by himself and cry. He said that he had never cried before. I really had to coax him to release his tension and fears through his tears. Finally, he walked away from us, and I could hear him crying. Our children, four and seven at the time, were playing by a stream and did not notice.

Stanley had remarkable focus. He continued to work obsessively. He endured each round of chemotherapy and radiation with courage and determination. The first new battery of tests showed improvement in his liver. This gave us hope. He remained positive for a long time. When he did not lose his hair with treatment, he fulfilled a lifelong wish to have a ponytail. This made him lighthearted. He got his happy walk back. There was a bounce to his gait again.

A trip to Lourdes, France, proved to be encouraging. Bathing in the miraculous waters added to Stanley's positive outlook. He brought home a two-gallon jug of holy water and blessed himself every day and swallowed his medications. He ate healthily and got lots of sleep. He continued to ski, golf and hike, which kept him strong.

We prayed together each night before we fell asleep. Our church community, as well as many friends and family members, were praying for a cure. The outpouring of support that Stanley received was amazing. If anyone was worthy of such affection, he was, as he had always been an extremely kind and generous person. Stanley was a physician who saved many lives.

After much thought and anguish he decided to have surgery that would be extensive and life altering. When we went to see the surgeon and schedule the date, the doctor said that he was not a candidate for the surgery. We left Memorial Sloan Kettering beaten. Stanley cried uncontrollably. We were in Manhattan and able to find a quiet restaurant where we talked and talked. He unburdened himself of a lot of his fears of death. He expressed remorse at leaving so young after working hard to have a successful career as a doctor. I told him what I came to believe through all my spiritual reading and journey. I explained that I believed through reading metaphysical books that we come into this world after we have chosen our parents and the experiences we are going to have. Which included his cancer diagnosis. I emphasized that we were souls traveling together. That is why we knew, when we met, that we would marry. There was something so familiar already. As Catholics, we are promised eternal life. Eastern religions believe in reincarnation. "There are lessons to be learned in our lifetime that we are destined to learn. We are grouped together to learn these lessons. I feel strongly that the two of us were meant to live through this together." He listened closely until I was finished and merely said "I hope that you are right."

Chemotherapy was on hiatus for a short time, so we went with our children to Disney World. Stanley lived with a lot of hope due to the great amount of support and our prayerful life. We had such a memorable time in Disney World! The children will always remember the time spent with their dad. I am so glad that we planned that trip when Stanley was able to enjoy it.

In December 2002 the scans showed massive new growths on his liver, and what originally became clear in the pancreas was back. At this point, Stanley was exhausted with the fight. He did not go to work anymore. He began to focus on model sailboats. He became absorbed in rigging those small sailing vessels. He did not want to see friends and family anymore; but of course, they wanted to see him. So, we had a two-hour gathering for a large number of family members for a Mass in our home. I remember before he came down to be with everyone he dressed in layers. A t-shirt, collared shirt, and then a big wool Irish sweater to appear healthier than he was. It was a difficult gathering for him because he knew it was really a goodbye. Stanley appeared to be at his best but slipped away and rested in the guest room. I think that he was really hiding in the hope that goodbyes were not exchanged. Some relatives did find him in the guest room but he pretended he was sleeping and avoided the goodbyes.

Most others wrote him beautiful, heartfelt letters expressing their love and gratitude for his life, good times and friendship. I think this was more therapeutic for the individual writing the letters than it was for him. Stanley let them pile up at his bedside. I saved them for the children to read to help them recall what a wonderful dad they had (from the perspective of others).

Those whom he did allow to visit were his mother, siblings and very close friends. One dear friend came twice a week and massaged him. We had a routine at the end of the night that we would sit by the lit fireplace. Not much talking. Just being...although he did share that he was "Seeing dead people all day long." "Oh," I said, "How was that?" "Pretty scary," Stanley said calmly.

Stanley's mother had a strong personality and he always was seeking her approval and love. One night during a visit with her he had an anxiety attack that he had never had before. She came down into the kitchen where I was with my sister and said "He needs you." He was in bed trying to catch his breath, hyperventilating. I sat with him and tried to talk him through it. His mother sat in a chair across the room. Stanley tossed in the bed without relief. I put a Xanax under his tongue. (This is usually a swallowed anti-anxiety medication.) I got into bed with him and body hugged him, and he became less agitated. His mother watched from the chair across the room. I thought she should leave, but then realized that she needed to see how we love. Stanley became calm, and we lay in each other's arms. I asked his mother to get the CD player from the basement and to play a CD of very calming sounds of the ocean that his youngest sister had given him. We continued to rest comfortably, but then he shot up and went into the bathroom and did not come out until his mother left. I asked him, "What happened between you and your mother?" He said, "My mother was just being my mother."

(Now, many years have passed and I have learned to love my mother-in-law. I believe at age ninety-two she has also learned to love as she approaches death and has become aware of her vulnerabilities and of those around her.)

The next day he was scheduled for a procedure called paracentesis. He had developed ascites, which is a buildup of fluid in his abdomen. This procedure withdrew five liters of fluid. This gave him much needed relief from pressure and pain. When we got home, he collapsed from exhaustion on the couch, unable to go up the stairs to the bedroom. The doorbell rang, and we could see that it was his mother. He said, "Do not let her in." He seemed to be so empowered at that moment. Something happened for him regarding his mother. I believe he finally realized that he was not going to get what he needed from her and thought about himself at that moment. Stanley came to terms with his mother's conditional love the day before he died. His lesson was to realize that he was lovable. It was something he had to learn in this lifetime. In his process of dying he did learn to trust me, his wife. He gave up control to me when he couldn't sustain the control any longer. He knew to his soul that I would care for him. Letting go of his lifelong resentment toward his mother freed him. He learned to create a boundary, he learned to trust, and he learned to surrender. And knew that I loved him.

At five in the morning the next day I woke with Stanley sitting at the side of the bed, and he gently said to me, "I am going to die today." I rushed around to him and hugged him for what seemed like an eternity. He said that he was sorry for leaving and I said that I would be all right. I promised to take care of our children. I gave him permission to die. He said "Thank you." We prayed the rosary together and he was able to recite forty of the fifty Hail Marys! I told him of my belief in the afterlife again just as I did twice before during his illness. Because of all my reading of metaphysical and Eastern philosophy, I talked about living lives together that we chose, our souls traveling together, and that there is no separateness. We will always be together in love. He said, "I hope you are right, I hope you are right, El." He asked me to administer more pain medication, and he drifted off to a deep sleep.

That afternoon I got a call from our lawyer, who was helping us with the necessary legal matters. As I left our bedroom and explained to Stanley what I was doing, he wanted to participate, still thinking that he could. I assured him that I could take care of everything. His brothers were with him, and my sister was in the kitchen. I left him in good hands.

While I was driving with the attorney and his wife, a thunderstorm ended, and I saw in the sky the largest rainbow that I have ever seen. Wierdly, actually extraordinarily, I squealed, "It is a sign, it is a sign!" They did not respond. He kept telling me the legal stuff. I repeated, "It is a sign, it is a sign!"

We took care of business, and I was home an hour and fifteen minutes after I'd left. My brother-in-law met me in the driveway and told me Stanley had passed away. Actually twenty-five minutes after I left. I was so shocked that it had happened without me! I ran up into the bedroom and slammed the door behind me, to be alone with my husband. The house was filled with friends and family. I was crying on his chest. Sounds came out of me that were like animal noises. I was thinking in my head, "How could you do this without me!" I was really angry with him for not waiting for me as I cried deeply on his chest. Then something remarkable happened. By telepathy, I heard "What about the rainbow?" With that I sat up, stopped crying, and looked at him, dead in our bed. And I thought, "I did hear you say that." The rainbow was a sign! With that the phone rang at the bedside. It was the lawyer whom I'd just left. He said, "Ellen, I know." I said, "What about the rainbow?" He wholeheartedly agreed. Sometimes things happen that you cannot understand rationally....

Also, it was March twenty-first. This was the anniversary of my niece Lindsay's death. My sister Tina had put on their tombstone the words "Somewhere Over the Rainbow." I truly feel that Tina and Lindsay were there to welcome Stanley and let me know, too. Days later, I shared this at his funeral, someone who had taken a picture of that huge rainbow gave it to me....

After the funeral my brothers and sisters went upstate New York to ski. We were together at the top of the mountain eating peanut butter and jelly sandwiches. Up until this point I had requested not to be left alone, and my siblings had obliged me. I suddenly decided to get up and go skiing. All of them got up too. I said, "Oh, no thanks, I am okay, I want to go alone." I assured them that I was okay. They were hesitant but allowed me to ski off by myself. This was the first time I was by myself in a very long time. I remember thinking that I felt good. I was skiing effortlessly on double diamond slopes. My "S" turns felt natural as I went down one trail and then the next, which opened up to a large open area. It was here that I heard Stanley, my husband, say to me in my deepest mind (not a voice), "You were right, El, it is beautiful here." And I just kept on skiing and said to him, "Thanks for telling me, Hon."

P.S. My mother-in-law has had a hip replacement after a fall. I went to visit her at home after rehab. Upon leaving I knelt down to hug her while she was seated in her cushioned chair. Embraced in the hug, she said to me, "Thank you, I need this." I hugged her for what seemed an eternity.

CHAPTER VI
IT'S REALLY JUST LOVE

I had a Jewish patient named Florence who was actually a strong hospice patient. Her melanoma had metastasized to her lungs, liver and adrenals. When we first met she had just stopped chemotherapy and was fatigued and emotionally exhausted. Sometimes hospice patients get better when the team arrives, which was the case with Florence. She recovered from the effects of her treatments and was feeling stronger. Her morale was up due to the regular visits of the hospice team. Also a 24/7 private hire was now living with her. There was no overt physical expression of the cancer. Although she was homebound, she ambulated on her own, was continent of urine and bowel, was eating a regular diet and enjoyed talking with whomever she allowed into her home.

Florence thought she was going to die soon because hospice showed up. I had to convince her that the hospice team does not hasten death. Hospice care is comfort care. Physical symptoms are cared for as they occur. Emotional and mental processes are considered, as is spiritual needs. In Florence's case she was clear that there were NO spiritual care needs for her.

Florence's condition was very stable. We were friendly, and I asked her permission to inquire about her Jewish upbringing. She explained that her grandparents were Orthodox. Her mother continued to be Kosher, using two sets of dishes, although her parents were not truly observant Jews. They just did it to do it. All the holidays were celebrated. Florence does not follow Kosher laws, but recognized the holidays. I asked her, "Where is God in that?" "God?" she said. "It's about tradition. There is no God for me."

"What about when you die?" I asked. "When I die, that's it. I'm ninety-two years old, I've lived my life. Although I'm very concerned about leaving my sister," she continued. "We are all we have." Florence was relieved when I explained that hospice bereavement support would continue thirteen months after her death for her sister. She then reflected about her mother. Florence's beautiful blue eyes looked wistful as she thought about her mother and expressed what wonderful persons her mother and father were. She continued at length with her wonderful memories of her Orthodox grandparents. I interrupted Florence and asked her if she felt God there. Gently, she said, "What?" "I believe God is love," I said. With bright eyes and a wide smile she said, "I'll buy that!"

CHAPTER VII
A MUSLIM PATIENT

I examined a male patient from Yemen for inpatient hospice. He came in for a chemotherapy treatment that could not be infused due to his abnormal blood counts. I thought we would need an interpreter, but when I walked up to him and his wife, they appeared eager to talk with me. His wife spoke for him. The conversation in English led to complete acceptance of hospice care. He looked at us with large sunken eyes. He was in a fetal position appearing very small in the bed, wool cap for warmth on his head (or was it to cover the baldness due to the effects of chemotherapy). "Thank you" was what he softly repeated several times when I told him he was eligible to go to the hospice.

The following day he was due to transfer. His wife dressed him. When I came into the room he sat uncomfortably in a chair grimacing, hunched over awaiting transport. Then the transfer was cancelled until the next day. They tried to conceal their disappointment. With great effort he was able to get back into bed. I apologized and he said "What does it matter whether I am in this bed or that bed?"

I was about to leave when he requested that I pray for him. Returning to the edge of the bed I asked, "Can I pray now?" His wife was waving her hands back and forth signaling "no" to me. Gently, he gestured to her and softly said, "It doesn't matter, it doesn't matter, we are all the same."

I began with the sign of the cross and recited the Hail Mary. Their eyes were closed and they were reverent. When I finished the Hail Mary without hesitation he prayed out loud in a deep voice in his native tongue with his hands clasped. I felt present in the moment. There was such a calmness throughout the room.

The next day he was transferred to hospice care. He was all bundled up on a gurney with his wool cap pulled below his ears. He appeared somber and was experiencing existential pain. The physical fight was over and the reality of death was in front of him. Normally, I do not go to the hospice. For this patient I had to go. His room was dimly lit and he was sleeping peacefully. Two people were at the base of the bed, we whispered and introduced ourselves. The young woman, his daughter, wore a hijab, a long scarf that covered her head but revealed her beautiful face. The young man introduced himself as the man's son and was dressed in J.Crew.

I mentioned to them that I prayed with their father the day before. I told them that I would never forget the experience. They looked at each other in shock. I continued, and said that their mother prayed also with us. "Oh no," his son said. "Our mother lives in Yemen." They giggled with bright smiles, witnessing my puzzlement. My patient had more than one wife. Their dad, a Muslim man, continued to sleep comfortably.

CHAPTER VIII
CATHOLIC GUILT

My godmother, "Aunt" Julie, was my mother's best friend. They met as teenagers in a club called the Daughters of Mary. Aunt Julie is ninety years old. She also lived her life devoted to the old school dogma of the Catholic Church, pre-Vatican II.

I visit her regularly, and often she brings up her past including things she has done of which she is not proud. She had spoken of these things to a priest in Confession. With much distress she admits that she has not been forgiven. I told her that she needs to go to confession with a different priest!!

Julie's husband, who was an abusive alcoholic who beat her and often humiliated her in public died decades ago, as have many of her friends. She endured much hardship. She was orphaned at age fourteen. She was unable to have her own children but adopted and raised two boys. She often wondered about death.

On one of my visits she told me that dead people were in her living room when she woke from slumbering in front of the television. Most are people she recognized. They do not harm her, but they did scare her. She wondered what they want. I think that they are inviting her to recognize another dimension, trying to help her realize that death does not have to be feared and that in death these loving entities are with us. They are all around us. She listened intently when I explained my views and she wanted to believe it. She knows she sees dead people!

On another visit, she said, "I don't understand. How is the world going to end? Will Jesus Christ come? Will all of us die at once?"

I try explaining Vatican II, which began in 1964, and states that we are all holy. By his death and Resurrection, God's son has saved us. At the end of time, Jesus Christ will come to fully establish God's Kingdom. The Holy Spirit is within all of us and emanates from us. We are not damned to hell.

We talked and talked and talked some more. Aunt Julie seemed very lighthearted. But before we went to bed the last thing she said was, "But I don't understand: how is the world going to end?"

Oy Vey!

P.S. A Jesuit priest from my parish visited her when she became homebound and absolved her of the things that were heavy on her heart. She believes that she is now prepared spiritually to die.

CHAPTER IX
A BEAUTIFUL JOURNEY

I worked as a nurse and *doula* for seven months for a seventy-two-year-old extremely wealthy woman named Gertie. Gertie was eccentric, obstinate, controlling, powerful, a passionate Democrat, mean, always right, generous, stubborn, open and giving, oddly, of herself. She was dying of breast cancer that had metastasized to her bones. She was in a lot of pain and required oral pain medication, as well as opiate patches. She was recovering from shingles, which gave her yet more pain. Pain management was key at this time in her life. Constipation management was crucial too. Once the constipation was treated, the nausea and vomiting subsided.

Although she did not overtly believe in God there was something quite spiritual about Gertie. She said if she were anything she was a Buddhist. Her connection to people, many people, at all times, young and old, culturally diverse, strange or normal, seemed to be her passion. Her home was always open. Most folks were welcome. (But, if she did not like you – you knew it.) In most cases the compassion and love she gave and received was a joy to watch.

Gertie's fears revealed she never wanted to be alone. When she woke, she looked for someone. I especially enjoyed our mornings together. She would whisper, and so would I. We whispered until she was fully awake.

She was tough. She liked to tell everyone what to do, and how to do it. These are just a few characteristics that she developed to hide her vulnerability. Gertie had a tumultuous, on again off again relationship with her two sons. As she neared acceptance of her death, she talked to me about her boys. She said, "Lester hasn't been mean to me." We were already discussing the older son's meanness. She expected me to say something…. "Oh," I said, "I wonder where they got that from." Gertie looked at me, meeting my eyes. We both knew where they got that from (her) and said nothing. We had a lot of alone time in which the atmosphere became very peaceful and Gertie seemed to go within. Her constipation and pain was finally well managed. She was eating very little: broth, Jell-O, mashed potatoes, clementine's, crackers with goat cheese, boiled eggs, coconut juice, water, toast and small amounts of various fruits. Over time, these became hard for her to eat too.

Gertie found God, or love, and peace and joy by simple things such as watching a male and female cardinal in her garden. A bird feeder brought more birds. Many, many other cardinals, doves, finches, and squirrels too. We had a huge super soaker water pistol to scare off cats. She was delighted with all the activity just outside her wall-length, floor-to-ceiling windows.

One day while watching the cardinals, Gertie drifted away and said, "Let's go to the barn across the meadow." She saw this vision a few times. I usually responded with silence and watched the peace in her face and the brightness in her huge blue eyes. Sometimes she insisted on a response from me, and I would simply say, "Have you been there before?" and she would continue to stare. As an individual gets closer to death, such visions seem to help them remember another time that was pleasant, either in this lifetime or another. Gertie would tell me that her deceased husband, Tom, was sitting at the end of the bed. Usually this happened in the morning. When she was closer to death, she mentioned his presence throughout the day. She also slept most of the time and woke only briefly.

Gertie became so exhausted from the fight and accepted the last leg of her journey to death when she became peaceful and loving and willing to accept love. She learned to trust. Caring for Gertie changed my life. Because by just being myself, this cantankerous woman let down her defenses, exposed her vulnerability, and accepted that death was near. She trusted that I would care for her as she entered this most feared part of life. I was honored.

CHAPTER X

PEACE

I was recommended by a hospice nurse to another family that wanted someone to stay with them for more than a brief visit. Actually, it was nine hours. But in those nine hours I was able to establish peace among the caregivers, who were panicking. The patient had already "made the turn." He was unable to swallow. Secretions were audible in his breathing. He was unconscious without response to physical touch. He had no bowel sounds, his kidneys were not producing urine, his hands and feet were mottling. Also, his blood pressure was no longer audible with the sphygmomanometer. His loved ones were open to any suggestions I could give. I believe the peaceful atmosphere we established gave the patient the rest and peace he needed to take his last breath.

Six months later his lover was dying of brain cancer. The in-laws, friends and extended family began to fight among themselves over the presumed well-being of the patient. I received a call to return to that address. I stayed for nine days. I met the patient who was alert and oriented. Because I was a stranger, upon my arrival she realized that this was it! She allowed me in. She accepted her fate. Within a day she lost consciousness.

I was at her bedside, and she appeared to be staring at me. But I could tell that she was not focusing on me but something else. She had a faraway look in her eyes, and she said out loud, "But, I don't know how to fly." One hour later a man came to the bedside as she was gently waving her right arm. This was her brother, who took her arm and held it close to him. I said softly, "Allow her; apparently, she is flying."

It is exciting to become involved with a family, getting to know the patient by listening to the loved ones. It is usually cathartic for each one of them. As the days became numbered and peace pervades, ill feelings slip away. Love fills the atmosphere as the individual slips into unresponsiveness. System by system slows until the last breath is achieved. All is well....

CHAPTER XI

A MOTHER AND ELDEST DAUGHTER

I met fifty-eight year old Zula in her hospital room calmly vomiting small amounts of feces (due to bowel obstruction). Her daughter, Ebony, was at the bedside with a large suitcase because she arrived from Texas. Ebony, always on her feet, reached for a suctioning wand to assist her mother. Zula had advanced cancer in her abdomen that had widely metastasized causing a small bowel obstruction. Her abdomen was distended and very taut. She was no longer eating or receiving any type of intravenous nutrition. Her pain was not controlled. She ordered Ebony around and Ebony followed her mother's every command.

The following day Zula was no longer vomiting. I met her partner, Henry, who said that Zula could move mountains. She came to the United States with two small children from Africa. Her first husband stayed behind not having the curiosity or bravery needed to leave their country. Zula made a good life in America for herself and two children before meeting Henry. Henry and Zula had a daughter together, Stephanie, who was eighteen, bright eyed, beautiful, very confident, and accepting of the hospice atmosphere. I believe that she was confident because they were all together. Zula's family, her partner and children were a united front as Zula lay dying.

We were all together in a large private hospital room. Zula was in and out of consciousness and free from pain. Henry was recounting her herculean bravery and controlling personality that he loved so much. Stephanie was politely agreeing. Ebony wholeheartedly agreed in a most loving manner. Zula tried her best to respond. Everyone giggled with delight that she was still trying to control. Madio, the health care proxy, on the other hand, was not laughing. Rather, he wanted to know what would happen next. He was keeping everything in order. I explained the active dying phase that Zula had entered. The family stayed together keeping vigil.

The next day Ebony was alone with her Mom and waved for me to come in. Ebony was trying to convince her mother that there was not a hole in the center of the bed. Zula said she was falling and she wasn't ready. Ebony frantically smoothed the sheets and bed pads to prove there was no hole. As I stood quietly at the bedside, it appeared that Ebony was doing what she had always done, which was to try to please her mother. Zula was trying to turn to the side of the bed where I was. She said "If I get on my side I can avoid it." At this point Zula did not have the strength to move onto her side.

What was happening in front of me caused chills to run up my spine. I motioned to Ebony to stop smoothing the sheets. She appeared relieved with my assistance. I asked Zula, "What is there?" She said, "a big black hole and I'm falling." I said, "It's okay, you can let go." Zula replied, "No, I can't, my children need me." "I can't leave my children." Her eyes were closed as she spoke. "Help me get on my side so I can hold on." I gestured to Ebony to pull the sheets which would allow her mother to roll onto her side towards me. Zula reached her hands out to me and grabbed my arms and actually had some energy to pull as Ebony rolled her. Zula wanted to grab onto the hospital railings to hold on. Hold on from "falling, falling, falling" she said peacefully. I repeated, "It's okay to let go." She said, "My children need me." Ebony locked eyes with me to give permission to encourage Zula to let go. I told Zula that I met all her children. I told Zula they are fine adults. I told Zula she did a great job as a parent. I told Zula she taught them her strength of character. I told Zula they will be okay. "You have taught them well." Zula's grip weakened from my arms and she became more peaceful. Ebony said, "Thank you, Mom." Zula rolled back to the middle of the bed and drifted off to a deep sleep. She died within twenty-four hours.

Zula will never leave her daughter.... This kind of love never dies.

CHAPTER XII

THE LOVERS

The care of Andre and Kiran was assigned to me from hospice. When I arrived at their apartment on the Upper West Side of Manhattan, they were very upset. The team from hospice explained that Andre had cancer of the blood and only six months to live. All medical intervention had been stopped. Kiran, however, said "BULLSHIT." They cancelled hospice care. We chatted all afternoon and met for breakfast the next day. Andre was from Madagascar and Kiran was born in India. They were an extremely interesting couple. Their shop of antiques from Africa and India had to be closed due to Andre's failing health. A huge closeout sale took place to liquidate their merchandise. Even with so much sold, their railroad apartment was lined with lovely artifacts from their respective countries.

I became intrigued with them both and continued to visit each week. They spoke about their childhoods with love and happiness. They would bicker frequently in my presence. Andre was deaf. He wore a device that allowed him to hear somewhat. When he was tired of talking, he would simply take it off. At times, Kiran would raise her voice and say, "Put on your ear!" At the same time she would be waving at her own ears to show him what she meant! Sometimes he would comply.

As time progressed, I sat privately with Andre, and he reviewed his life. Often a patient feels more comfortable speaking to a hospice team member, a stranger, rather than a loved one, about their life experiences. It can be very cathartic for the dying individual. All I have to do is listen. This is known as active listening. It creates a compassionate atmosphere.

After one such conversation, Andre asked me to buy Kiran her favorite flowers. She was not home at that moment. I returned with a bouquet of daisies. He pretended that he had gone out to get them (which would have taken great effort at this point). The two of them were so happy and expressed such love for one another; I cried when I left.

Six months later. Andre was in the hospital for yet another blood transfusion. Only this time he ended up on life support.

His kidneys had failed, and he was receiving dialysis. A resident doctor suggested to Kiran that the respirator be shut off. He felt that Andre would die naturally soon after. This was an excruciatingly painful decision for her to make. After hours of sitting beside Andre and then out in the waiting room while dialysis was performed again, she decided to "pull the plug." We stared at him, thinking his heart would stop immediately without the aid of the ventilator. He and Kiran both appeared peaceful. We spoke about him and laughed too. Many hours passed, and I went home. Kiran called at about two in the morning, and she was crying softly. She agreed to come to my home by cab after settling affairs in the intensive care unit. Together we watched the sun come up over the East River with a cup of tea. Kiran seemed to be in a state of bliss, then she slept very soundly.

Two years later almost to the day – Kiran died. I was called to identify her body at the Medical Examiner's Office. At age sixty-two, she joined Andre. They had no children. In her grief she began to use alcohol as a "solution." She had been a recovering alcoholic but had stopped going to AA meetings and calling her sponsor after Andre died. Her desire to join Andre was great. So she did.

CHAPTER XIII

GRIEF

Physically separating from loved ones takes extreme courage… but love continues. Remember the "inseparableness" of love in the grieving process. I have found myself praying for the death of a loved one for the relief of their suffering. I once felt guilty about this but since realized it is an expression of profound love that can be shared for each other. Still, the loss of friendship or companionship causes deep sorrow. But heartache can also bring awareness of another dimension. In my grieving process, the loss of the friendship I had with my sister, Tina, was keen. The comfort of having parents was lost. The levels of intimacy gone with my husband have not been recovered. Over time, I have bonded with others to fill these voids, but not until I had felt all the pain. I had to embrace the losses and grieve, then I was able to move on to have healthy new relationships. Having friends of all ages is important.

DYING PERSONS GRIEVE FOR THEIR LOSSES UNTIL RIGHT BEFORE ACCEPTANCE….

Being safe, feeling safe with someone to talk about your journey to death is so important. A friend, a family member, a hospital staff member, a member of the clergy, or a volunteer from the hospice team. When a dying person is able to articulate their present moment a release of energy occurs, which brings acceptance and peace followed by love. Finding the right confidant is key. The conversation may have the feel of a confession. Facing disappointments in one's past behavior or judgment and choices needs to be expressed and let go. The person listening should not judge but only listen. Perhaps some gentle advice can be given when the patient has shared their memories.

Life is a process. I have found like-minded friends. I used to share my experiences with the supernatural with some who would then question me at length, leaving me feeling as though I was defending that which is true for me. I stopped sharing with these individuals. When I meet people who have had these experiences or who are open to that, meaningful interaction is possible.

Through friends I meet more friends and have more like-minded conversations and interactions. So, now I have a community of loving friends from whom I receive comfort and to whom I give comfort. This is love.

During my own painful processing of grief my parish pastor met with me regularly and allowed me to vent my anger. He was the only one who accepted this outpouring of raw emotional anger, which was so important. I believe I frightened others who then stayed away after witnessing my distress. My pastor stuck with me and would even argue back. He kids me now about it, and we both smile.

When hospice is entered, someone has accepted the truth of looming death. This may be the family physician, the dying individual, a member of the family, or a friend. With hospice, the pressure is off the family. The fight is being won. It is all about love.

…It is really okay. Why? Because there is no time! Because "It's beautiful here," said my husband five days after his death telepathically as I skied.

Love is a vibration…an energy.

Love will never die.…

HELPFUL REFERENCES

- A Living Will gives instructions for medical treatment after you can no longer communicate/Choose a Health Care Proxy.
- Last Will and Testament.
- Funeral arrangements/Cremation.
- As the end stages of death are approaching the patient is withdrawing. When treatments stop, keeping the outside world out feels comfortable. Fatigue/weakness takes over. Staying home feels safe. Typically the patient only wants close friends and family at home. (Someone may have to be the "bad guy" and say no to visitors who aren't in this inner circle, although they may think they are!)
- Create a quiet, peaceful environment.

- The dying person sometimes needs to be left alone and in silence.
- When he or she wants to talk JUST LISTEN.
- Be present. Acknowledge that you hear them.
- Try to adjust the level of pain relief so that there is comfort. No concern of addiction at this time.
- Avoid constipation. Drink prune juice, daily colace and senokot, miralax powder, lactulose or dulcolax suppository.
- The bedroom will become a safe haven.
- Bedbound: personal care should be done by a family member who is comfortable doing this or someone privately hired. Turning and positioning avoiding bed sores, applying skin lotion and giving mouth care are important.
- At some point fear of death is gone. Death is welcomed…acceptance, peace and love.
- You can't prevent anyone from dying.
- Appetite decreases slowly and texture of food has to be easily swallowed (i.e., yogurt, applesauce, pudding, Jell-O, Ensure, ice cream, thickened fluids (buy Thick-it at the pharmacy/it's a powder). If coughing occurs upon swallowing - NO MORE.

- The goal is a peaceful comfortable death. Every family has its own dynamics which are good, bad or indifferent.

- Offering food is a loving act. Accepting food is a loving act. But when it becomes more harmful than good and aspiration (food falling into the lung) may result - food must be stopped.

- Feeding tubes and IV fluids are not natural and are an insult to a slowing, slowing, slowing physical process. Third spacing will manifest.

- Chemicals are released from our bodies at this point aiding in the slowing down process which act like endorphins. ACTIVE DYING PHASE is unfolding.

- Unconsciousness occurs.

- Please assume that the dying person can hear, even though they may be unconscious (don't argue, gossip or talk about medical stuff).

- This is a good time to give your loved one permission to die. Express that you will be alright and will care for those around the patient (children, parents, pets).

- The goal is a peaceful comfortable death (2nd mention). Try not to blame each other or project onto each other the gravity of the situation.

- Low dose morphine is given sublingually for breathing pattern changes and for pain. This does not hasten death (that's a myth!).

- Using a fan to gently move the air in the room is far more helpful than oxygen nasal cannula. The trigeminal nerve of the face is activated by the fan which assists in comfort.

- Urine decreases.

- Restlessness or agitation most often occurs and usually occurs at night (terminal restlessness/agitation). Ativan or haldol can relieve this end of life symptom.

- What are perceived to be hallucinations also occur and are commonly deceased loved ones who support, comfort and assist in the journey. This is often exhibited by a gently waving of the hand or calling them by name.

- Secretions become obvious (terminal secretions or "death rattle"). This is not painful. Turning from side to side, and elevating the head of the bed will aid in draining these secretions somewhat. Medication can also alter the further production of secretions (atropine, glycopyrrolate or a scopolamine patch).

- The goal is a peaceful comfortable death (I purposely say this again). You will reflect later and be glad that you exuded patience. Take a deep breath. Go for a walk.

- Dying is a natural process, as natural as childbirth. You wait for a child to be born and we wait again until death comes.

- Frequently the dying will wait to die until their loved ones have left the room.

- The feet will become cold, the toes will become purple followed by mottling of the balls of the feet.

- Remember: A personality is a personality and remains until the last breath.

- Love and experiences you had with your loved one will live on, after death, in your mind and heart. The evolving soul is present – the physical body dies.

- Love never dies....

PRAYER/RITUAL REFERENCES

- Christianity
- Islam
- Judaism
- Buddhism

I am not an historian nor a priest. I hope the prayers and rituals presented here provide a guide for patients and loved ones in a difficult time. I do not intend any disrespect to any religion. I do not profess to be a master of any religion.

CHRISTIAN PRAYERS

INDULGENCED PRAYER TO ST. JOSEPH TO BE SAID
ESPECIALLY AFTER THE ROSARY
ASPIRATIONS FOR THE DYING

PRAYER FOR A HAPPY DEATH

O GLORIOUS ST. JOSEPH, behold I choose thee today for
my special patron in life and at the hour of my death. Preserve
and increase in me the spirit of prayer and fervor in the service
of God. Remove far from me every kind of sin; obtain for me
that my death may not come upon me unawares, but that I
may have time to confess my sins sacramentally and to bewail
them with a most perfect understanding and a most sincere
and perfect contrition, in order that I may breathe forth my
soul into the hands of Jesus and Mary. Amen

ANOTHER PRAYER FOR A HAPPY DEATH

O BLESSED JOSEPH, who yielded up thy last breath in the arms of Jesus and Mary, obtain for me this grace, O holy Joseph, that I may breathe forth my soul in praise, saying in spirit, if I am unable to do so in words: "Jesus, Mary and Joseph, I give Thee my heart and my soul." Amen.

ISLAMIC PRAYER

THE QUR'AN

Chapter Al-Baqara, verse 156

Inna Lillahi wa inna ilayhi raji'un. Inna lillahi wa inna ilayhi raji'un

We belong to Allah and to Allah we shall return.

JUDAISM PRAYER

END OF LIFE PRAYER

Vidui

My God and God of my ancestors, Author of life and death, I turn to you in trust. Although I pray for life and health, I know that I am mortal. If my life must soon come to an end, let me die, I pray, at peace. If only my hands were clean and my heart pure! I confess that I have committed sins and left much undone, yet I know also the good that I did or tried to do. May my acts of goodness give meaning to my life, and may my errors be forgiven. Protector of the bereaved and the helpless, watch over my loved ones. Into Your hand I commit my spirit; redeem it, O God of mercy and truth.

One also recites:

Shema Yisraeil, Adonai Eloheinu, Adonai echad. Baruch shem kavod malchuto l'olam va'ed.

Hear O Israel, Adonai is our God, Adonai is one. Blessed is God's glorious name now and forever.

BUDDHISM TEXT / MEDITATION

San Francisco Zen Center

HEART SUTRA

Heart of Great Perfect Wisdom Sutra Avalokiteshvara Bodhisattva, when deeply practicing prajña paramita, clearly saw that all five aggregates are empty and thus relieved all suffering. Shariputra, form does not differ from emptiness, emptiness does not differ from form.

Form itself is emptiness, emptiness itself form. Sensations, perceptions, formations, and consciousness are also like this. Shariputra, all dharmas are marked by emptiness; they neither arise nor cease, are neither defiled nor pure, neither increase nor decrease. Therefore, given emptiness, there is no form, no sensation, no perception, no formation, no consciousness; no eyes, no ears, no nose, no tongue, no body, no mind; no sight, no sound, no smell, no taste, no touch, no object of mind; no realm of sight ... no realm of mind consciousness. There is neither ignorance nor extinction of ignorance... neither old age and death, nor extinction of old age and death; no suffering, no cause, no cessation, no path; no knowledge and no attainment. With nothing to attain, a bodhisattva relies on prajña paramita, and thus the mind is without hindrance. Without hindrance, there is no fear. Far beyond all inverted views, one realizes nirvana. All buddhas of past, present, and future rely on prajña paramita and thereby attain unsurpassed, complete, perfect enlightenment. Therefore, know the prajña paramita as the great miraculous mantra, the great bright mantra, the supreme mantra, the incomparable mantra, which removes all suffering and is true, not false. Therefore we proclaim the prajña paramita mantra, the mantra that says: "Gate Gate Paragate Parasamgate Bodhi Svaha."

Meditations on Loving Kindness and
Compassion for the Very Sick and Dying

Extracts from Facing Death and Finding Hope by Christine Longaker,
Random House, New York, 1997.

LOVING KINDNESS MEDITATION

One of the hardest things about suffering is the feeling that we are trapped in our painful circumstances – lost, hopeless and alone. We fear our suffering will go on forever, and that there is no way out of it. And when we don't know how to transform or heal our own suffering, we may find it difficult to be with and support others in distress. Before we can extend compassion toward others, we must first feel love. If we find our own heart is wounded or walled up, the Loving Kindness Meditation can help reconnect us to the source of love within. Once this love opens our heart and heals our pain, then we will be able to offer our genuine love and fearless compassion to others.

Sit quietly, and let all the scattered aspects of your mind and energies settle down. Acknowledge and embrace gently any suffering or struggle that you become aware of.

Now, remember a person from your life who once loved you very much. Imagine this person sitting in front of you at this very moment, extending his or her love to you once again. It's alright if you can recall only one happy memory with the person – make that memory of love your entire experience and bathe in its healing warmth.

Feel the other person's love coming towards you like rays, warm rays of sunlight, permeating your entire being, and especially filling and warming your heart. If there is an old barrier around your heart, see it not as a massive or impenetrable wall, but as a fragile or thin layer of ice. Let the love flowing toward you melt the ice of your old hurt or fear, warming and nourishing your heart.

As this healing love comes into you, you feel your heart overflowing with love and gratitude. You feel peaceful, whole and replenished with love. Naturally, your love and gratitude now goes out to the person who evoked it, wholly and unconditionally.

Once this giving and receiving of love is flowing strongly, expand the direction of your love another degree. Imagine that your friend who is in pain or who is suffering and dying is in front of you. Extend the same love to them, fully and joyfully. See your love as white light/ nectar and send it straight to their heart, filling them with peace and happiness. Feel that their whole body becomes peaceful, pure white light, and that they can rest in joy and peace, at least for a few moments.

If time is short, you can finish the meditation here and dedicate the positive merit you have generated to all sentient beings, wishing that they may quickly reach their full and complete potential.

Otherwise, continue and consider now that on either side of this central person are other people in your life whom you love and cherish, and extend the same love to them, fully and unconditionally. Then extend your love to encompass even those you don't know very well: co-workers, shopkeepers, neighbors, even strangers you pass on the street. Expanding your love further, visualize that in front of you are those who irritate you, those you've been angry with, or those who seem to be your enemies. Extend the same love to them, fully and completely, loving and accepting them exactly as they are.

Finally, expand your love to embrace all beings. Consider now that the whole space in front of you is filled with beings throughout the universe, all forms of conscious life, including the tiniest insect, and even those who have died. Now your love is boundless and unbiased, and it shines powerfully onto each and every one, extending happiness to all existence.

As you conclude this practice, don't shake off the inspiration, awareness, or limitless love it has aroused. Instead, as much as you can, continue practicing the essence of this meditation throughout the day, extending unconditional love firstly to yourself but at the same time toward everyone you meet.

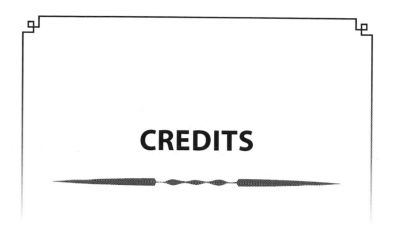

CREDITS

Cover page: Sculpture by Antonio Canova

Christian Prayers: Fr. Dennis Yesalonia

Islamic Prayer: Imam Ahmet Atlig

Judaism Prayer: Rabbi Sam Kastel

Buddhism Meditation: hayagriva.org.au / San Francisco Zen

Center: Heart Sutra

MESSAGES FOR LOVED ONES

ADDITIONAL RESOURCES

I am sharing these books that I have read because
they have informed and nourished my thinking:

Al-Anon Members. *Hope for Today* (Virginia Beach, Virginia:
Al-Anon Family Groups 2002)

Alexander, Eben. *Proof of Heaven* (New York: Simon &
Schuster 2012)

Bennett-Goleman, Tara. *Emotional Alchemy* (New York:
Harmony Books 2001)

Braden, Gregg. *The Divine Matrix* (California: Hay House
2007)

Browne, Sylvia. *Journey of the Soul Series* (Carlsbad, California:
Hay House 2000)

Byrne, Rhonda. *The Secret* (New York: Atria Books 2006)

Carlson, Richard. *Don't Sweat the Small Stuff...and it's all small stuff* (New York: Hyperion 1997)

Chopra, Deepak. *How to Know God: The Soul's Journey Into the Mystery of Mysteries* (New York: Penguin Random House Audio, Narrated by Deepak Chopra, M.D. 2000)

_____. *Metahuman* (New York: Harmony Books 2019)

_____. *Twenty Spiritual Lessons for Creating the Life You Want* (New York: Harmony Books 1995)

Covey, Stephen R. *The 7 Habits of Highly Effective People* (New York: Simon & Schuster 1990)

Coelho, Paulo. *The Alchemist* (New York: HarperCollins 1993)

Day, Dorothy. *The Long Loneliness* (New York: HarperCollins 1952)

De Meester, Conrad. *The Power of Confidence* (New York: Alba House 1969, 1995)

DeMello, Anthony. *Awareness, The Perils and Opportunities of Reality* (New York: Doubleday 1992)

Dowling Singh, Kathleen. *The Grace in Dying* (New York: HarperCollins 1998)

D'Souza, Tony and Wonsiewicz, Bud, *Discovering Awareness, A Guide to Inner Peace, Strength and Freedom* (Canada: Broadband Living Press 2006)

Dyer, Wayne. *Wishes Fulfilled* (New York: Hay House 2012)

Edward, John. *One Last Time* (New York: Berkley Books 1999)

Frankl, Victor E. *Man's Search for Meaning* (Boston, Massachusetts: Beacon Press 1959, 1962, 1984, 1992, 2006)

Gerrard, Nicci. *The Last Ocean: A Journey Through Memory and Forgetting* (New York: Penguin Press 2019)

His Holiness The Dalai Lama and H.C. Cutler, M.D., *The Art of Happiness, A Handbook for Living* (New York: Riverhead Books 1998)

His Holiness The Dalai Lama - Translated and Edited by J. Hopkins, PhD., *How to See Yourself As You Really Are* (New York: Atria Books 2006)

Keating, Thomas. *The Human Condition, Contemplation and Transformation* (New Jersey: Paulist Press 1999)

Keyes, Jr., Ken. *Handbook to Higher Consciousness* (Kentucky: Living Love Publications 1975)

Kübler-Ross, Elisabeth. *On Death and Dying* (New York: Macmillan 1969)

Lavenia, George. *What You Think is What You Get* (New York: The New Earth Foundation 1997)

Lewis Paulson, Genevieve. *Kundalini and the Chakras* (Woodbury, Minnesota: Llewellyn Publications 1991)

MacLaine, Shirley. *Out on a Limb* (New York: Bantam 1983)

_____. *Dance While You Can* (New York: Bantam 1991)

Merton, Thomas and Edited with an Introduction by W.H. Shannon. *The Inner Experience* (New York: HarperCollins 2003)

Moorjani, Anita. *Dying To Be Me* (New York: Hay House 2012)

Nhat Hahn, Thich. *Anger* (New York: Riverhead Books 2002)

_____. *The Energy of Prayer* (Berkeley, California: Parallax Press 2006)

_____. *Fear* (New York: HarperCollins 2014)

_____. *The Heart of the Buddha's Teaching* (Berkeley, California: Harmony Books 1998, 2015)

Ostaseski, Frank. *The Five Invitations, Discovering What Death Can Teach Us About Living Fully* (New York: Flatiron Books 2017)

Poitier, Sidney. *The Measure of a Man* (New York: HarperCollins 2003)

Redfield, James. *The Celestine Prophecy* (New York: Warner Books 1994)

_____. *The Tenth Insight* (New York: Warner Books 1996)

_____. *The Celestine Vision* (New York: Warner Books 1997)

_____. *The Secret Of Shambhala* (New York: Warner Books 1999)

Rolheiser, Ronald. *The Holy Longing, The Search for a Christian Spirituality* (New York: Doubleday 1999)

Ruiz, Don Miguel. *The Four Agreements, A Toltec Wisdom Book* (San Rafael, California: Amber-Allen 1997)

_____. *The Mastery of Love, A Toltec Wisdom Book* (San Rafael, California: Amber-Allen 1999)

Saint Therese of Lisieux, Edited by Mother Agnes of Jesus, *The Story of a Soul* (Rockford, Illinois: TAN Books 1951,1997)

Sharma, Robin S. *The Monk Who Sold His Ferrari* (New York: HarperCollins 1999)

Thurman, Robert A.F. (translated by) with Foreword by His Holiness The Dalai Lama. *The Tibetan Book of the Dead* (New York: Bantam Book 1994)

Tolle, Eckhart. *The Power of Now* (Vancouver, Canada: New World Library 2003)

_____. *Stillness Speaks* (Novato, California: New World Library 2003)

_____. *A New Earth* (New York: Penguin Audio, Narrated by Eckhart Tolle 2005)

Verploegen Vandergrift, Nicki. *Organic Spirituality* (New York: Orbis Books, Maryknoll 2000)

Weiss, Brian L. *Many Lives, Many Masters* (New York: Simon & Schuster 1988)

_____. *Messages from the Masters* (New York: Warner Books 2000)

Williamson, Marianne. *A Return to Love* (New York: HarperCollins 1992)

_____. *The Gift of Change* (New York: HarperCollins 2004)

Weber Long, Stephen. *Caring for People with Challenging Behaviors* (Baltimore, Maryland: Health Professionals Press 2005)

Wilson, Bill. *Twelve Steps and Twelve Traditions* (New York: Alcoholics Anonymous 1952, 1953, 1981)

Zukav, Gary. *The Dancing Wu Li Masters* (New York: HarperCollins 1979)

_____. *The Seat of the Soul* (New York: Simon & Schuster 1989)

Zukav, Gary and Linda Francis. *The Heart of the Soul. Emotional Awareness* (New York: Simon & Schuster 2001)

ACKNOWLEDGEMENTS

My children are my source of great love. My husband, siblings, and parents are always with me. With appreciation and love to Ken, Gail, Leslie, Kari, Steve, Karen, Issan, Laura, Matty, Vanessa, Lori, Kathy, Maureen, Stephen, Jay, Patrick, Fr. Frank, Carlos, Scott, Romaine, Fr. Michael, Ginny, Anthony, Mary, Virginia, Britta and Barry for their guidance and edits of this manuscript.

I have much gratitude to the patients and families who allow me into their sacred space.

I am honored....

For discounted bulk book sales contact:

Channel Sales - Content Distributors LLC

Toll free: 812-339-6000 ext. 5022

OR

Email: channelsales@authorsolutions.com

Printed in the United States
by Baker & Taylor Publisher Services